A Picture Book of

BUTTERFLIES and MOTHS

Written by Joanne Mattern
Illustrated by Roseanna Pistolesi

Troll Associates

SWALLOWTAIL BUTTERFLY

The long, pointed "tails" on its wings give this butterfly its name. These tails look like the long wings of a bird called the swallow.

Swallowtails live all over the world, except for the frozen lands of the Arctic and Antarctic. Some live in wet marshes. Others like dry fields.

Like many butterflies, Swallowtails like to drink sweet *nectar* from flowers. They sip it through their long, hollow tongues. As they fly around the flowers, Swallowtails pick up bits of powdery *pollen* from one flower, and leave it on another. This helps make new plants grow.

Library of Congress Cataloging-in-Publication Data

Mattern, Joanne, (date)
  A picture book of butterflies and moths / written by Joanne Mattern;
illustrated by Roseanna Pistolesi.
      p.   cm.
  Includes index.
  Summary: Describes the appearance and behavior of a variety of
butterflies and moths.
  ISBN 0-8167-2796-1 (lib. bdg.)   ISBN 0-8167-2797-X (pbk.)
  1. Butterflies—Juvenile literature.   2. Moths—Juvenile
literature. [1. Butterflies.   2. Moths.]   I. Pistolesi, Roseanna,
ill. II. Title.
QL544.2.M28   1993
595.78—dc20   92-5225

EASTERN TAILED BLUE BUTTERFLY

This butterfly lives in fields and gardens. It lays its eggs on clover, beans, and wild pea plants. That way, when the eggs hatch, the caterpillars will have plenty of their favorite food nearby.

LITTLE YELLOW BUTTERFLY

The Little Yellow likes warm weather. In the summer, this butterfly is common in the northern United States. But when the weather gets colder, it must fly south or it will die. This trip from one place to another is called *migration*. Butterflies migrate because they cannot keep themselves warm. Their bodies are the same temperature as the air around them.

MONARCH BUTTERFLY

Every fall, Monarch butterflies go on a fantastic journey. They leave their homes in Canada and the northern United States and fly south to California, Florida, Texas, and Mexico, where it is warmer. When spring comes again, the Monarchs migrate back north. This trip can be as long as 2,000 miles (3,220 kilometers)!

As the Monarchs fly north, they lay eggs on the milkweed plant. These eggs hatch into caterpillars. As the caterpillars grow, their skins become too small for them and have to be shed. This is called *molting*.

After a couple of weeks, the caterpillar molts for the last time. Its body turns into a hard shell called a *chrysalis* (KRIS-ah-lis). Inside, a great change called *metamorphosis* (met-ah-MORE-fo-sis) is taking place. When the chrysalis cracks open about 2 weeks later, the caterpillar has become a butterfly.

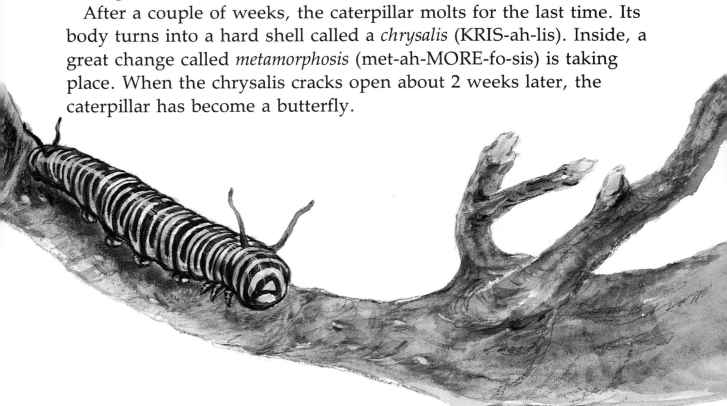

RED ADMIRAL BUTTERFLY

The Red Admiral is part of a group of butterflies called *brush-footed butterflies*. All butterflies have 3 pairs of legs. But brush-footed butterflies only use 2 of these pairs for walking. Their front legs are very short and covered with hairs. These hairs are very sensitive. They help the butterfly tell when nectar is nearby.

COMMA BUTTERFLY

The small, white, comma-shaped marks on the bottom of its wings give this butterfly its name. The Comma lives near orchards and gardens, where it can feed on fruit that has fallen from the trees.

ZEBRA LONGWING BUTTERFLY

When the sun sets, groups of these butterflies land on branches. Here they sleep through the night. When morning comes, they fly away, looking for nectar to drink.

Zebra Longwings are very colorful and easy to see. Birds like to eat butterflies, but they leave Zebras alone. They know that Zebras taste bad. Its unpleasant flavor keeps the Zebra safe.

CABBAGE WHITE BUTTERFLY

When this butterfly is ready to lay her eggs, she flies from one plant to another, smelling each one with her *antennae* (an-TEN-ee). She is looking for a cabbage plant. When she finds one, she lays her eggs on a leaf. About 10 days later, tiny caterpillars, or *larvae* (LAR-vee), hatch from the eggs. They eat the cabbage leaves and grow bigger, until it is time to change into butterflies.

APOLLO BUTTERFLY

Most insects fly by flapping their wings. Not the Apollo! These butterflies spend a lot of time floating on the wind with their wings held straight out. Because they often live high in the mountains, Apollos are sometimes called ''the king of the mountain.''

Apollos are different from most butterflies in another way. Most caterpillars change into butterflies after only a few weeks or months. But the Apollo grows very slowly. It may be 2 years or more before the caterpillar is ready to make its chrysalis and turn into a butterfly.

PEACOCK BUTTERFLY

If you've ever seen a bird called a peacock, you know it has large, colorful spots on its tail. The Peacock butterfly has the same sort of spots on the inside of its wings. That's how it got its name.

The Peacock butterfly hides from enemies by folding its wings up. The dull, dark outside of its wings makes it hard to see the butterfly when it rests on a branch or tree trunk.

LUNA MOTH

How can you tell a moth from a butterfly? There are 4 ways. The best clue is the time. Butterflies are active during the day, but moths come out at night. The other differences are in their bodies. Most butterflies have thin antennae with knobs on the end, and thin, hairless bodies. Moths often have thick, feathery antennae, and their bodies are fat and furry. They also spread their wings out when they are resting, while butterflies hold their wings up in the air.

The Luna moth is often seen in the eastern part of the United States. Its pale green color and long wings make this one of the prettiest moths.

PUSS MOTH

The Puss moth's fluffy body looks like it is covered with cat fur. That is how the Puss moth was named.

A Puss moth caterpillar has an interesting way of scaring away *predators*, animals that want to eat it. It pulls its head back and lifts the front of its body to show a bright red ring and 2 black spots. This looks like a frightening face, and tells most predators to keep away.

SILKWORM MOTH

Silk is one of the most delicate and beautiful fabrics. And it is made by caterpillars! When the Silkworm caterpillar is ready to turn into a moth, it spins silk from its mouth. Then it wraps the silk around its body to form a *cocoon*. If you unwind the cocoon, you will have one long piece of silk.

UNDERWING MOTH

The dark wings of this moth are hard to see against the tree bark. But if an enemy comes too close, the moth opens its wings to show a pair of colorful wings underneath. This scares the enemy and gives the moth time to fly away.

Moths are *nocturnal*. That means they sleep during the day and are busy at night. When darkness comes, the Underwing wakes up and begins to look for food.

TIGER MOTH

Have you ever seen
a woolly bear caterpillar?
These fat, furry caterpillars
are actually the larvae of the
Tiger moth.

Birds and lizards won't eat Tiger
moths because they are poisonous. The hair on the
woolly bear caterpillar is also poisonous, and can even bother
a person's eyes or skin.

IO MOTH

Those large, dark circles on the Io's (EYE-ohs) wings are called *eyespots*. Many butterflies and moths have them. When a bird or other predator comes close to the Io, the moth flashes its eyespots. This usually frightens the animal away and saves the Io from becoming a tasty dinner!

INDEX

Green-Backed Skipper Butterfly